Listen, Whispers the Baobab

About the Author

Swarn Lamba is a passionate and creative individual known for her storytelling abilities and deep appreciation for nature. With a keen interest in wildlife and environmental conservation, she draws inspiration from the beauty and complexity of ecosystems, particularly highlighting the lives of plants and animals, such as the majestic baobab tree. Through vivid imagery and thoughtful narratives, Swarn aims to educate and inspire others to cherish and protect the environment.

As a talented author, Swarn also explores cultural themes in her writing. Among her notable works are "Let's Play - Kanche and Other Traditional Games of India," which showcases the rich tapestry of Indian games, and "A Twinkle a Tear: Moments in a Mother's Life," a poignant narrative that delves into the complexities of emotions. With her passion for connecting readers to diverse cultures and experiences, Swarn continues to inspire through her storytelling.

Listen, Whispers the Baobab

Tales from the Tree of Life

Swarn Lamba

Illustrator: Noah Cail

ZORBA BOOKS

ZORBA BOOKS

Published by Zorba Books, December 2024
Website: www.zorbabooks.com
Email: info@zorbabooks.com
Author Name: Swarn Lamba
Copyright ©: Swarn Lamba
Cover Image Artist: Akilimali Abdalah

Title: Listen, Whispers the Baobab

Printbook ISBN: 978-93-5896-460-8
Ebook ISBN: 978-93-5896-153-9

Zorba Books Pvt. Ltd. (opc)
Sushant Arcade,
Next to Courtyard Marriot,
Sushant Lok 1, Gurgaon – 122009, India

Printed by Manipal Technologies Limited
A1 & A2 Shivalli Industrial Area Manipal Udupi, Karnataka – 576104

A mystifying journey
Of an Africa that gave
And an Africa that took
Stories untold, journeys unfold
The emotive mysterious African continent

– Swarn Lamba

Dedication

To my children Jay and Mansi,
who grew up in Tanzania, their first home,

To my beloved granddaughters, Hana and Riya,
May you one day roam the vast landscapes of Tanzania,
where the whispers of the baobab echo stories of
resilience and life.

May you embrace the beauty of this land,
where every sunset paints a memory and every creature
tells a tale.

Carry the spirit of this place in your hearts,
and know that you are forever connected to its wonders.

Contents

Preface

For as long as I can remember, I have felt a deep connection to the beauty and complexity of nature. The lush landscapes, vibrant wildlife, and the majestic baobab tree, with its sprawling branches and ancient wisdom, have always called to me. This book is a culmination of my journey—a heartfelt homage to the land I have cherished for 36 years.

The baobab tree, standing tall as a sentinel of time, embodies resilience and strength, qualities that resonate deeply within me. Through its whispers, I have discovered a rich tapestry of life and an understanding of our interconnectedness.

This book is my way of giving back to the land that has given me so much. It is a tribute to the delicate balance of our ecosystems and the importance of preserving them for future generations. I hope to inspire readers to cherish and protect our planet, recognizing that every creature, no matter how small, plays a vital role in the grand narrative of life.

As you turn the pages, may you hear the whispers of the baobab and feel the heartbeat of the earth. Join me on this journey of discovery, and together, let us celebrate the beauty of nature and the stories it has to tell.

Acknowledgments

I would like to express my heartfelt gratitude to my beloved granddaughters, Hana and Riya, whose curiosity and wonder about the world inspire me every day.

I am immensely grateful to Sheila Mallia for being my sounding board and providing invaluable feedback during the drafting and editing process.

I would also like to acknowledge Noah Cail for the wonderful illustrations and for facilitating this journey to publication.

A special thanks to Muzu Sulemanji and Prema Lalji in Tanzania, who believed in me.

I must also mention the International School of Tanganyika, which provided me the opportunity to connect with the late Graham Mercer. His writing, stunning photography, and evocative stories have been a great inspiration to me.

Lastly, to all the readers who find joy and meaning in these pages, thank you for joining me on this adventure. May the whispers of the baobab resonate in your hearts as they do in mine.

Chapter 1

I Am the Baobab

I am the Tree of Life, Mother of the Forest. A towering giant, resilient and majestic—I am the Baobab.

More than just a tree, I am deeply rooted in the local culture and the ecosystem. I am known as the *Mbuyu* tree, at home in Tanzania.

Many a man and beast have rested against my trunk and in my shade. Many a bird have built their nest on my branches. Many are the stories I have heard and many are the scenes I have witnessed. 'Come, sit around me and listen... listen'.

Chapter 2

***

Here I Stand

Here I stand, proud and tall, even when the sky darkens with ominous clouds and the wind swirls dust into the air, snapping branches, howling, crying, and baying like a wolf in the night. Fearlessly, I remain unmoved as lightning splits the sky and thunder reverberates through Tarangire. Sometimes the rain falls gently like a spray; other times it pours as if buckets of water are unleashed from the heavens. Animals seek refuge, moving closer and closer to me, for I am the mother of the forest. When the skies lighten and the sun re-emerges, they will roam again, but during storms and droughts alike, I remain steadfast. In times of severe drought, when animals come searching for water, I provide and protect.

Standing over 20 metres tall and more than 10 metres wide, I reign majestically in the dry, open woodlands of Tarangire National Park. Around me, trees and vegetation have flourished for years, though none as long as I have, sharing the landscape. I witness the endless cycle of life—old trees withering away as new ones take root. Nearby, thorny thickets of graceful acacia trees stretch out, their flat tops adorned with long, straight thorns or hook-shaped ones to ward off browsers. In the distance, I glimpse occasional palm trees, dense patches of elephant grass, and ribbons of riverine forest winding through the land.

Not far away, vast swamps sprawl, lush with reeds and grasses that become impassable during the rainy season but remain green and vibrant throughout the rest of the year. When the rains come, wildflowers bloom in a vivid display of colour, making my home even more breathtaking. Tourists eagerly capture the scene with their cameras, striving to preserve the fleeting beauty of this wild, untamed landscape.

I love being here, rooted in one of the most popular game reserves in Tanzania. Tourists travel from all over the world to experience the wonders of Tarangire. Some come for the wildlife, others for the birds, and a few come to admire plants and trees like me. I have no idea how I came to be here—perhaps a seed from my ancestors was carried by the wind or dropped in an animal's droppings, landing here where I now stand. Around me, other baobabs grow, and I wonder if any of them are my parents or ancestors. I am a mysterious tree; no fossils of my kind have been found, and I do not generate rings in my trunk to mark the passing years. How long have I been here? 50 years? 100 years? 1,000 years? Or more? I cannot say...

Chapter 3

Haraka Haraka Haina Baraka (Haste Has No Blessing)

I grow slowly because I am in no hurry; I have many, many years to live. Most of the year, I am without leaves as I need to conserve the water I have. I look rather odd with the finger-like green leaves that appear during the wet season. They grow on me for only three months of the year; otherwise, I would lose too much water through them, and that is scarce around here. When the leaves fall, you can see my thin, spindly branches reaching upward and outward toward the blue sky. My thick, bulbous trunk is my big belly that stores gallons of water. My bark and flesh are soft, fibrous, and fire-resistant. My roots extend farther than my height. I don't sway or whistle with the wind like the graceful palms do. I simply stand in the background, providing a setting and bearing witness to ever-changing history.

I remember my first flowers blooming when I was probably 20 years old. Every year since, dozens of heavy, white flowers, drooping down on long stems the size of saucers, blossom on me. Each flower has five petals that are leathery and hairy on the inside, with a large number of stamens. The flowers open at sunset. With their musky odour, they attract fruit bats and hosts of other tropical insects. The bats and insects feed on the sweet nectar from my flowers and help with pollination. Once satisfied, they move on. My tired and drained flowers, after offering their hospitality, do not live for long. The sweet-scented flowers soon emit a carrion smell as they turn brown and suddenly topple to the ground, lying dead. I will have to wait another year before their beauty graces me once more, welcoming back my visitors.

As I wait through the long year, my flowers give way to seeds encased in furry pods. The olive-green, velvety coat gradually hardens into a tough shell. This is the only fruit in the world that dries naturally while still attached to the tree. It ripens for six months, during which time the pulp dries completely. Even after being plucked, the *mbuyu* fruit, as it is known in Tanzania, can last for up to three years.

Chapter 4

❦

My Guests

"*Wageni mwakaribishwa*" (guests are welcome). It would be shameful for guests to leave hungry, as that goes against the culture where I live. I'm a silent witness to the comings and goings of countless creatures. Some seek shelter in my shade, while others come for nourishment, and a few simply pass by, leaving behind a trace of their presence.

Baboons, mischievous vervet monkeys, warthogs, and elephants love the sour taste of my *mbuyu* fruit—as do humans!

The baboons come in large troops, and not far behind are the vervet monkeys. They are very noisy, chattering and squabbling loudly as they leap from branch to branch. They run up and down my trunk and branches with amazing speed, teasing and playing with each other. They make use of every part of me—the sturdy branches for resting, the hollows in my trunk for hiding, and the fruit I bear during the season. Their dexterity is unmatched, and

I've seen them pluck fruit from my branches with ease, biting into it greedily. Sometimes, the bigger baboons and monkeys snatch fruit from the smaller ones, making them run screaming to their mothers. Their antics are harmless, and I enjoy their liveliness. The quieter ones, after having their fill of fruit, sit and groom each other, while others fall asleep in my branches. I once had a vervet monkey that fell asleep and toppled off the branches—that was not a good way to be woken up!

During the hotter hours of the day, I often find the zebras gathered in my shade. Their black-and-white stripes form a mesmerising pattern against the golden grass, and their soft, high-pitched braying fills the air. They stand quietly, tails flicking to keep the flies away, resting before continuing their endless search for fresh grazing. Sometimes, I overhear their discussions—how they must remain vigilant, always watching for the lions lurking in the distance. They trust me to provide them with protection from the heat, and I am happy to offer it.

At dusk the elusive bushbuck and impala tiptoe carefully around me, though they tend to stay away from the vervet monkeys and baboons, who climb all over the bushbuck's back. Thankfully, bushbucks don't eat the fruit; otherwise, the vervet monkeys would be snatching it from their mouths. The bushbuck, with their large eyes and graceful legs, are always on alert, listening for the slightest rustle in the bushes. Their presence brings a certain calmness to the evening, as they nibble on the grass and stand beneath my branches.

I watch the wildebeest as they graze on the open plains around me, their shaggy coats flickering in the golden light of the dry season. They travel with purpose, driven by the search for water and fresh grass near the Tarangire River. Occasionally, they pause to rest under my branches, their snorts and grunts breaking the silence. But they never stay for long, always alert to the lurking lions and hyenas, and soon they are off again, continuing their journey across this wild landscape. The Maasai refer to wildebeests as *sifuri ubongo*—"zero brains" in Swahili. I don't agree; I think they are quite smart. They travel thousands of kilometres in search of food and return when it is green again.

The giraffes are my tallest visitors, and I admire their grace and calm demeanour. They move with such elegance, towering over most other animals, but they do not tower over me. They delicately pick at the leaves of the trees around me, their long tongues curling around branches with expert precision. Though they rarely feed on my leaves, preferring the acacia nearby. They often pause beneath my branches, their enormous eyes blinking slowly. With a swing of their necks, they easily get rid of the primates climbing on them. Like from a catapult, the primates are thrown far. The giraffe's neck is its most powerful, manoeuvrable weapon, and they certainly know how to use it. I wonder what they see from so high up, perhaps glimpsing far-off places I'll never know.

In the distance, I can see a herd of elephants headed my way. They are my most frequent visitors. The matriarch, wise and knowing, often leads the herd to me. She stands beneath my branches, her wrinkled skin illuminated by the setting sun. They're magnificent, large yet graceful, and they treat me with a curious mix of respect and destruction. Their trumpeting grows louder as they approach. No one really wants to mess with the elephants. The elephants in Tarangire are bigger and live in larger herds than those in other parts of Tanzania. The bushbucks slink away, while the baboons and monkeys climb to the highest branches. Some run away, only to return when the coast is clear. When I was younger, I was afraid of the elephants too. As they press their massive heads against my trunk, I can feel their low-frequency rumbles as they communicate with each other. They know where I store my water, ripping my bark with their tusks and chewing on the soft, pulpy wood to quench their thirst. Sometimes, they chew right through to the other side, leaving big holes. They've made some trees look as though their mouths are open in a scream.

When elephants attack younger trees with ferocity—tearing branches, devouring leaves, and stripping bark to reach the moisture—the trees can be knocked down, injuring or even killing the elephants. However, we are sturdy trees and can regenerate our bark, even after it has been ripped away.

I catch a glimpse of a leopard darting past, its sleek body moving with precision as it chases its prey. Leopards usually make their homes in the densely wooded parts of the park, but I have occasionally had the honour of hosting them. They are stealthy, solitary hunters who prefer the cover of darkness. When they seek refuge, they climb my sturdy limbs after a successful hunt, their golden eyes glowing faintly in the dim light. Sometimes, they rest on my branches, their spotted coats blending effortlessly into the shadows as they drape themselves with grace. I watch them lie still, breathing steadily, their ears twitching to every sound.

Rare for me to see are the gigantic hippopotamuses, who prefer to wallow in the swamps, only venturing out when the dry season forces them from their hiding places.

During the rainy season, when the swamps are full, warthogs often come by, snuffling around the roots and grasses near me. Their comical appearance with their tusks and short legs hides their intelligence and survival skills. They dig at the earth, searching for roots and bulbs, and their tails stick straight up like flags as they trot away at the slightest hint of danger. I've watched their families grow, generations of warthogs taking shelter near me.

I have seen many more—buffaloes, with their massive horns and powerful builds, come to rub against my trunk, their itchy hides relieved by my rough bark. The mongoose, scurrying about in search of food, darting between the roots of the trees. Even the porcupines, with their quills bristling, cautiously move through the underbrush at night.

They are all a part of a grand story—one that I am proud to be a part of.

Chapter 5

The Simba Roars

It may seem deceptively quiet during the day, but if you listen—truly listen—you'll find that it's rarely silent. Baboons holler and chatter, hyenas cackle with mocking laughter, wildebeests honk loudly, drowning out all other sounds, zebras bray, elephants trumpet, buffaloes bellow, and Simba—the lion—ROARS! When the lion roars, everything else falls silent, and all movement ceases. I too feel the tension. Lions pass me by, walking stealthily with their heads held high as they survey their kingdom, the true monarchs of the savannah. The males, with their thick manes, command respect, while the lionesses, strong and cunning, keep a watchful eye. On hot days, they rest in my shade, alongside lionesses and their cubs, alternating between play and snooze. I swell with pride to shelter them, knowing soon they will roam once more, hunting to provide for their families.

Lionesses do most of the hunting, working together to bring down larger prey like buffaloes, while the males protect the pride and cubs from threats, such as rival males or other predators. Their diet mainly consists of herbivores like zebras, wildebeests, impalas, and buffaloes. The abundance of wildlife in Tarangire ensures a steady supply of food, although during the dry season, hunting becomes more challenging as prey scatters in search of water.

The lions are adaptable, making the most of the park's ever-changing environment. In the wet season, they stay close to the Tarangire River and Silale Swamp, which draw in prey. When the dry season comes, they follow the migratory herds, moving to areas where food is more plentiful.

But life here isn't without competition. Lions often clash with other predators, like spotted hyenas, leopards, and cheetahs. Hyenas, notorious scavengers, sometimes steal kills from lions and vice versa, leading to fierce confrontations. Despite their strength and dominance, lions must always stay vigilant, especially when food is scarce.

Not long ago, a lioness dragged her kill beneath my shade, feasting with her family. I could hear the crunching of bones as they devoured the meal, and the scent of the carcass lingered for days. The blood of the impala soaked into the dry earth, and though I dislike the taste of blood that reaches my roots, it's part of life here. Soon enough, the hyenas approached, waiting at a safe distance to scavenge the remains, while vultures circled above, eager for their turn to pick at the flesh.

Lions, with their power, grace, and social dynamics, are truly the rulers of the landscape, embodying the raw, untamed spirit of the African wilderness.

<h1 style="text-align:center">Chapter 6</h1>

— ❋ —

The Beautiful *Ndege* (Birds)

Every day, I watch the skies above me, and I am never alone. Birds of all shapes and sizes grace my branches, some resting, others stopping just for a moment before continuing their journey. From sunrise to sunset, I am witness to their ceaseless activity and am part of their lives in ways even they may not realise.

At dawn, the first visitors to arrive are usually the yellow-collared lovebirds. They gather in small, noisy flocks, their bright green and yellow feathers flickering like the early morning sun through my leaves. These tiny birds, full of life and chatter, add a playful energy to the quietness of the morning. They nest in hollows of trees like mine, and I take pride in sheltering their families.

As the day progresses, I see the elegant lilac-breasted rollers with their stunning plumage of blues, purples, and greens. They swoop down from the sky, performing aerial acrobatics to catch insects mid-flight. Their beauty is unmatched, and when the sun catches their wings, it is like watching pieces of the sky itself dance.

Perched high on my branches, often silhouetted against the African sky, are the mighty martial eagles. With a wingspan that commands respect, these hunters watch the plains below with sharp eyes, waiting for the perfect moment to strike. When they do, it's swift and powerful—just as the lions on the ground stalk their prey, these kings of the sky reign supreme.

But it's the African fish eagles that often catch my attention from the far distance. They sit patiently near the Tarangire River, watching the water intently. Their piercing call echoes across the park—a sound that, to me, has become as natural as the wind. I can spot their white heads glinting against the deep blue sky, and when they dive for fish, the precision of their movements is breathtaking.

One of my favourite visitors is the vibrant superb starling. These striking birds with their shimmering blue-green and orange bodies flit around me, darting from one branch to the next. Their colours are like little jewels that stand out even in the golden light of the savannah. I've seen them pluck insects from the air or the bark, always busy, always moving.

Then there are the white-backed vultures, who soar on thermal currents high above, watching the land for the next opportunity. They rarely stop to rest on my branches, but when they do, their hulking presence is undeniable.

As dusk approaches, I often hear the haunting call of the African wood owl. It's a soft hoot that seems to signal the end of the day, a reminder that while the sun may set, life continues in the darkness. This owl, with its cryptic plumage, is almost invisible during the day, but under the cloak of night, it becomes a master of stealth.

In the distance, I sometimes catch a glimpse of kori bustards—the heaviest birds capable of flight. These ground-dwellers aren't frequent visitors to my branches, but I watch as they walk with measured steps across the plains, heads held high, scanning for insects and small reptiles. Their grace, despite their size, always amazes me.

During the rainy season, my branches become even more crowded. The weaver birds arrive in large numbers, and their incessant chattering fills the air as they weave intricate nests that dangle from my limbs. They are master builders, using twigs and grass to create homes that sway with the wind but stay sturdy and strong.

And then there are the hornbills—with their large, curved beaks and playful antics, they are hard to ignore. The red-billed and yellow-billed varieties are frequent guests, and I often chuckle to myself as I watch them toss fruit into the air, catching it with their long beaks.

My favourite time is when the eggs begin to hatch. I love the sounds of chirps, tweets, and hoots coming from little fledglings. Soon, they start falling from their nests and learn to spread their wings, leading to flapping that turns into flight. I feel proud to see them soaring in the sky, knowing they were raised under my protection.

The birds and I have a special bond. They bring life and music to my days, and I offer them a place to rest, a sanctuary amidst the vastness of the savannah. Each one, from the tiniest lovebird to the majestic eagle, plays a role in this ecosystem. I marvel at their resilience, their ability to thrive in this harsh, beautiful land, just as I have done for centuries.

I stand rooted to the earth, but through the wings of the birds, I feel connected to the sky, soaring through the air with them, witnessing the ever-changing world from their eyes.

Chapter 7

The Hidden Life Within

I, the venerable baobab, stand as a silent witness to the bustling life that thrives within and around me. Among my thick, weathered bark and expansive branches, a myriad of small creatures finds refuge, creating a vibrant ecosystem that enriches my existence.

Among my most fascinating inhabitants are the snakes. The graceful green mamba often weaves through my branches, its emerald scales glistening in the dappled sunlight. This snake, both beautiful and deadly, prefers the cover of my leaves as it hunts for unsuspecting birds and small mammals. In my hollow trunk, the stout rock python makes its home, coiling comfortably in the cool, dark interior. These serpents, while often feared, play a crucial role in the balance of nature.

As dusk settles over Tarangire, my branches become a haven for scorpions and nocturnal insects. The scorpions, with their menacing pincers and curved tails, find safety in the crevices of my bark, ready to defend themselves if threatened. They may seem intimidating, but they serve an essential purpose in my environment, helping to control the populations of smaller insects. As night deepens, I can hear the soft rustle of beetles and the gentle hum of moths drawn to the faint light filtering through my leaves. These creatures, often overlooked, play vital roles in pollination and decomposition, helping to sustain the vibrant life around me.

Even the tiniest of inhabitants, like ants, find sanctuary within my bark. These industrious little workers march up and down my trunk, forming colonies and sometimes even tending to their own aphid farms, while protecting my surface from pests. In return for their labour, I provide them with nectar from my blossoms, forming a symbiotic relationship that benefits us both.

Spiders weave their webs, trapping the little insects that come their way. Bees buzz busily around their hives. Through the countless creatures that dwell within me I witness the intricate web of life that surrounds me. Each creature, no matter how small or seemingly insignificant, contributes to the ecosystem's richness. I take pride in being a shelter and sustenance provider for them. I embrace all who call me home, celebrating the interconnectedness of our lives.

Chapter 8

In the Stillness of the Night

'*Lala Salama*,' says a mother in the nearby village as she tucks her child in for the night, and soon the village falls into peaceful silence. My neighbourhood, however, comes alive with a symphony of natural sounds, offering a sharp contrast to the daytime stillness.

In the distance the powerful, echoing roar of lions reverberates through the air—the most iconic sound of the African night. Male lions roar to signal their dominance, establish territory and communicate with their pride. Their majestic calls often heard from miles away, adding a primal intensity to the night.

The eerie, cackling "laugh" of spotted hyenas fills the air as they hunt or scavenge. Their whoops and giggles are a constant reminder of the wildness that surrounds me, as they roam in search of food.

Elephants, abundant in Tarangire, communicate with one another through deep, resonating rumbles that sometimes are felt as much as they are heard. Their occasional trumpets pierce the stillness, reminding me of their presence as they move through the park.

A constant backdrop of insect sounds—cicadas and crickets—creates a soothing hum that underscores the night. Their rhythmic chirps form the base layer of the nocturnal soundscape in Tarangire, a calming background in an otherwise wild setting.

Owls, nightjars, and the African wood owl make haunting calls through the darkness. Their hoots, whistles, and trills lend a mysterious and, at times, calming atmosphere to the night. Meanwhile, bats emerge, darting through the shadows as they head towards the baobab flowers, drawn by their nocturnal bloom and sweet scent.

Far away, near the Tarangire River and Silale Swamp, I can hear the distinctive grunts and snorts of hippos. Although they spend their days cooling off in the water, they come ashore at night to graze, and their vocalisations are loud and unmistakable.

During the wet season, I am not particularly fond of the croaking of frogs. Their loud, repetitive calls echo through the marshes and ponds, often lasting all night long, contributing to the park's nocturnal chorus.

The high-pitched cries of bush babies, small nocturnal primates, occasionally ring out. Their calls resemble a baby's cry, adding an eerie, plaintive note to the night.

Even the zebras, often docile, add to the cacophony with their high-pitched, barking calls that resemble laughter. These braying sounds are common as they communicate with each other and stay alert for lurking predators.

Occasionally, I hear the deep, rasping growls of leopards as they move stealthily through the night. These solitary big cats are rare to hear, but chilling when their presence is known.

Sadly, among the sounds of nature, I sometimes hear the sharp crack of gunshots—a haunting sound that brings a sombre note to the park's beauty, a reminder of the ever-present threat of poachers.

Together, these sounds—from the gentle hum of insects to the ferocious roars of lions—is the essence of the wilderness that surrounds me here in Tarangire.

Chapter 9

···◆···❋···◆···

My *Rafiki* (Friend) Tonkei

Ever so often the lean and tall Maasai warrior, Tonkei, walks toward me with his springy strides. He looks grand in his red *shuka*- the red symbolising his culture and the belief that it scares away lions. Around his wrists, ankles, waist and neck are beaded bands. Each colour of bead represents something- red means bravery and strength, blue represents the colour of the sky and rain, white shows the colour of a cow's milk, green symbolises plants, orange and yellow mean hospitality and black represents the people.

The lions and the maasai maintain a respectful distance from one another. There was a time when it was considered a rite of passage and a symbol of strength and power, for the young Maasai to go armed with spears and kill a lion. When they returned they were treated with respect by the tribe.

Fearlessly, the Maasai walk with their cattle, who follow with gentle obedience, traversing endless miles.

The cattle provide milk, blood, and meat for him and his family. He plunges his spear into the ground, almost puncturing my roots. Balancing on one foot, with the other braced against the inner thigh of the supporting leg, he stands in a heron pose, watching over his grazing cattle. I feel fortunate to hear him sing songs he has learned from his elders. Often, Tonkei is joined by another Maasai, Leboo, who also comes to graze his cattle.

"Sopa," Leboo greets him.

"Ipa," replies Tonkei.

I listen to the soft, rhythmic conversations as they speak in low, melodic tones, discussing their cattle—the lifeblood of their community.

They speak the Maa language and share stories of distant relatives, upcoming ceremonies, and the health of their livestock, keeping me updated with the news.

"We need to move closer to the water. The dry season is coming early, and the grass is fading," comments Tonkei.

Their connection to the land and nature runs deep and occasionally I hear them, offering thanks to the land and the spirits of their ancestors.

"Look at this baobab," remarks Tonkei, resting his hand on my trunk. "Strong, just like our people."

And I swell with pride.

"Ole Sera!" they say when Leboo leaves, meaning "go in peace."

Tonkei stretches his spindly arms to pluck the fruit from my branches, cracks it by hitting it with his spear, and eats the white, powdery, sweet-tart coating of the seed. The hard, black, kidney-shaped seeds are spat out around me.

Chapter 10

My Gifts for the People

In the heat of the dry season, I, the mighty baobab, watch as my fruits, called *Mbuyu,* ripen and fall to the ground. My fruit is not just any ordinary fruit; it is a gift to those who know its value. It is eagerly gathered by those who know their worth. I hear mothers teaching their children how to crack open the tough exterior to reveal the white, chalky pulp inside. They often mix it with water to make a refreshing drink, rich in vitamin C, to ward off illness. This drink is more than a thirst quencher; it strengthens the body, especially for those walking under the intense Tanzanian sun.

Some elders prefer to grind the pulp into a fine powder and sprinkle it over their meals, adding a sour, slightly sweet flavour to their food.

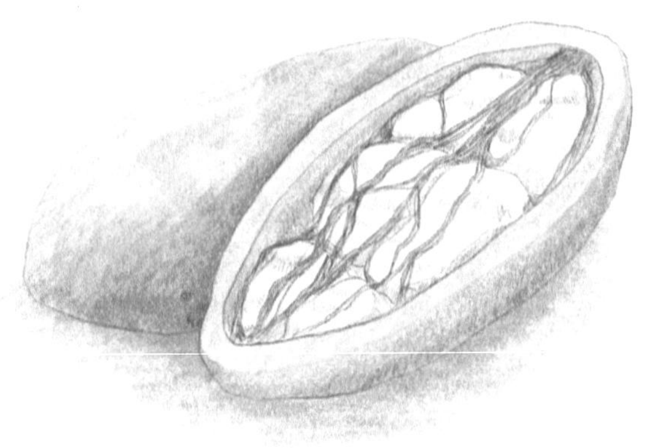

My seeds, hidden deep within the fruit, are just as valuable. People roast them, turning them into delicious snacks, or press them to extract oil. This oil, prized for its healing properties, used to nourish skin and hair, keeping them soft and healthy. Sometimes, they are even ground into a paste for medicinal use. When the village celebrates, they make candies from my fruit, coating the seeds in sugar and spices, and sharing my *Mbuyu* as a special treat for the young ones.

My leaves, though less celebrated than my fruits and seeds, are also harvested with care. During the rainy season, when they are lush and green, they are plucked and cooked as a vegetable, rich in nutrients. People believe that my leaves help fight disease and restore strength to the weary.

I am more than just a tree. I am a provider, a healer, and a source of sustenance.

Chapter 11

❖❖

Here Come the *Mtalii* (Tourists)

I hear the rumble of Land Rovers in the distance, carrying tourists eager to see me. Guides take pride in showing me off, the largest and most majestic baobab in the area. Sometimes, they arrive on foot, their eyes wide with wonder, or I see hot air balloons floating overhead, filled with people eager to capture me in their photos and videos.

One day, a lady on a bush walk with a Maasai guide leaned her cheek against me, wrapping her arms around my trunk as she sobbed, as though someone were tearing her insides apart like the elephants do mine. I let her stay until she was spent and could cry no more. When she finally looked up with renewed composure, she whispered a soft "thank you" and blew me a kiss before leaving. I felt maternal in that moment, deeply gratified to have helped her find some solace. I wish for people to have my sturdiness, strength, and resilience. Do not let life's hardships destroy you. Heal, repair, and regenerate, as I do.

Once, a young couple jumped out of a Land Rover and carved a heart with an arrow, etching their names within it and promising to return one day.

On another occasion, a busload of tourists disembarked and held hands around me to measure my girth. It took nearly all the passengers to encircle me while the tour guide kept an eye out for dangerous animals lurking in the bush.

Some people simply jump off the bus, give me a quick hug, and then hop back in. "*Heri yako heri yangu*" (Your happiness is my happiness), I say.

While I love the presence of people, I am not pleased when I have to breathe in the polluted exhaust fumes from tourist buses, Land Rovers, and safari vehicles. The harsh smell lingers long after they've left, tainting the air we all rely on, affecting not just me but all the plants and animals in the park.

The noise from vehicles, tourist groups, and even hot air balloons disturbs the natural tranquillity of my home. These sounds are foreign to us and cause stress, unsettling the peaceful rhythm of the wild.

Sometimes, tourists leave behind litter—plastic bottles, bags, food wrappers, and drink cans. Monkeys and baboons play with the discarded items, shredding the bags and kicking the cans. The wind carries the plastic bags, and they often get stuck in my branches, fluttering like unwanted flags for days. Birds and smaller animals can get entangled in them. The litter spreads!

I love welcoming those who come to admire me, but I hope they remember to treat my home with respect—for it is not just mine but theirs as well.

Chapter 12

Poachers' Hide

I dread the nights when I hear gunshots. The poachers are out again, like white chicken in the village, disrupting the tranquillity. They have evolved from hunting on foot with spotlights to using large vehicles and motorcycles, slaughtering animals for bushmeat, skins, tusks, and horns. After killing the animals, those on motorcycles bring small trucks to haul the carcasses away. Ruthlessly they tear out the tusks and sever the horns, leaving the wounded elephants and rhinos writhing in agony. The heartrending cries of the animals echo through the night and cast an eerie and sorrowful silence in the darkness of the jungle. The number of animals continues to dwindle, while the greed of humans only grows.

In the southwest of Tarangire, I've been told, stands an ancient baobab tree—massive and hollowed out by elephants and the elements. This grand tree was tragically repurposed by poachers into a hidden lair. To outsiders, it appeared as just another towering baobab, its entrance cleverly camouflaged with bark and wooden planks, concealing the secret activities within. The hollow chamber inside, nearly 10 metres wide, was used not only as a hideout but also as a butchery. Here, the poachers strung up the carcasses of wildebeests, zebras, and buffaloes, leaving them to dry. The interior was littered with the bones and skins of their kills, while the pungent smell of drying meat lingered in the air.

High up in the tree's branches, the poachers had built a crude lookout post, offering a panoramic view of the surrounding landscape. From this vantage point, they could scan for park rangers or scout out their next targets—giraffes, antelopes, and even elephants—all while remaining concealed within the embrace of the mighty baobab. On some nights, the poachers lit small fires inside the hollow trunk, the flicker of flames reflecting off the curved walls, turning the ancient tree into a den of predators.

For many months, the poachers operated undetected, using the baobab as their base. They carefully covered their tracks, ensuring no signs of their hideout could be seen from a distance. But the whispers of suspicious activity spread, and the park rangers began a thorough investigation. One fateful evening, after days of tracking footprints and tyre marks, the rangers closed in. They surrounded the baobab under the cover of darkness, capturing the poachers and putting an end to their slaughter.

Though the criminals were caught, the baobab could never recover from the dishonour of being used for such a purpose. Once a silent guardian of the wilderness, the tree now bears the name Poachers' Hide, forever marked by its grim history. Tourists flock to see it, curious about its story, but the baobab sags with shame, its hollow interior echoing with the memories of violence and betrayal.

Chapter 13

***

Oh, the Stories I Hear!

The conversations I hear are fascinating, and I am always learning. As the saying goes in Kiswahili, *Elimu haina mwisho* (Education has no end).

There are many myths and legends across Africa that try to explain how I came to be. Some of these stories are as ancient and wondrous as I, the Baobab.

One such legend comes from the people of Madagascar, where the baobab is deeply revered. It is said that when the world was new, the baobab tree was among the most beautiful of all trees, but it was vain and boastful. It admired its own reflection in the waters and would demand more sunlight than any other plant. The gods, irritated by the tree's arrogance, decided to teach it humility. They uprooted the baobab and planted it upside down, with its roots in the air and its branches deep underground. That's why, even today, the baobab looks like it has roots reaching for the sky.

In other regions of Africa, the baobab is believed to be the first tree created by the gods. According to some legends, when the Creator planted the baobab, it was so eager to grow that it shot up too quickly, becoming crooked and misshapen. Upset by this, the Creator yanked it from the ground and threw it across the land, where it landed upside down. Yet despite its strange appearance, the baobab was given the gift of longevity, enduring for thousands of years and becoming a symbol of resilience and survival.

The San people of Southern Africa tell another story. They believe that the baobab was one of the very first creations, given the task of holding up the sky. The gods gave the tree immense power and longevity, allowing it to grow for hundreds, if not thousands, of years. But as the tree grew taller and taller, it began to challenge the gods, trying to take over the heavens. In a moment of frustration, the gods grabbed the baobab and thrust it upside down into the earth, where it has remained ever since—its roots seemingly suspended in the air, reminding all of its attempts to reach the divine.

According to the African bushman, the god Thora took a dislike to the baobab growing in his garden, so he threw it over the wall of Paradise onto Earth below. Although the tree landed upside down, it continued to grow.

There are also more practical beliefs woven into these tales. Many communities in Africa see the baobab as the

Tree of Life, not just for its physical offerings like food, water, and shelter, but also as a spiritual symbol. It's thought that ancestors' spirits dwell within the baobab's trunk, and it is often the site of village rituals and ceremonies. People come to the baobab seeking blessings, healing, and wisdom from their ancestors.

One terrifying story told by a tourist from the Middle East was that the devil plucked the baobab and thrust its branches into the earth, leaving its roots in the air. Thankfully, I have not seen anything resembling a devil in Tarangire.

A mother once explained to her children, "The baobab tree was among the first trees to appear on land. Next came the slender, graceful palm tree. When the baobab saw the palm tree, it cried out that it wanted to be taller. Then the beautiful flamboyant tree appeared with its red flowers, and the baobab became envious and wished for blossoms. The fig tree was the next to catch the baobab's eye, and it prayed to bear fruit. The gods grew angry at this demanding tree and pulled it up by its roots, replanting it upside down."

Yet another legend states that when the baobab was planted by God, it kept walking and refused to stay rooted in one place like all the other trees. To stop its wandering, God uprooted it and replanted it upside down.

Even in the distant land of the Aboriginal people of Australia, there is a story about my origin. There, I am known as Baob, the bottle tree, or *larrkardiy*. They say I was once a graceful, proud tree, delighting in boasting about my beauty to the less elegant trees and plants around me. Frustrated, they all complained to God. He listened and decided to teach me a lesson for my arrogance by making my seeds sprout upside down

Yet another story recounts that God called together all the animals of the world. They stood in a long queue, and God gave each one a tree to plant as part of a campaign he was working on. The greedy little hyena, unable to part with the flesh she was eating, arrived late. She received a small baobab tree. Unappreciative of her gift, she flung it over her shoulder, causing the little baobab to land with its branches in the ground and roots in the air.

Most stories about my origin depict me as upside down. I look at myself—my huge trunk, spindly branches, and deep roots. I may appear different, but I am proud to be me. I am resilient, surviving where little else can thrive. But for how long, I wonder…

Chapter 14

My Africa, My Home

I stand tall and ancient, my gnarled trunk and sprawling branches holding the wisdom of centuries. Across Africa, I am revered not just as a tree but as a sacred symbol of life and spirituality. In many communities, my presence is woven into their stories and rituals.

Elders teach children the significance of my presence, sharing tales of how I have witnessed their history and the ebb and flow of life in the land.

In some cultures, I am known as the "Tree of Life," embodying the spirit of resilience and survival. People gather around my massive trunk for ceremonies, seeking my strength as they pray for good fortune, health, and abundant harvests. My hollowed trunk sometimes serves as a sacred space, where offerings are made, and the whispers of ancestors are believed to flow through my branches.

Beliefs have been passed down from generation to generation. Some tribes say that if a baby boy is bathed in water infused with baobab bark, he will grow up strong; however, bathing him for too long may lead to obesity! Others believe that drinking water in which baobab seeds have been soaked will keep you safe from crocodile attacks. I often wonder if anyone has ever sent a boy, bathed in infused water, to a crocodile after giving him a drink made from soaked baobab seeds.

In some tribes, marriages take place under the baobab trees like me. They also believe that eating a baobab flower will lead to being eaten by a lion. Some tribes bury their ancestors beneath the trees, while others believe that spirits residing under the trees haunt the living. People come to these trees to ask the gods for permission to hunt; without the baobab's blessing, the hunt is believed to be unsuccessful. The tree serves as a place to request everything—from protection and food to marriage and health.

In South Africa, one hollow space was transformed into a pub. Known as the Sunland Baobab, this tree is one of the largest and oldest baobabs, with an estimated age of around 1,000 to 6,000 years before it split in half in 2017. The most incredible story I've heard is of a hollow trunk being used as a prison!

In Senegal, a country in Africa, the baobab appears on its coat of arms. What an honour that is!

I have heard that near a place called Keren in Eritrea, there is a massive baobab tree that houses a small church called St Mary's.

In Zimbabwe, there is a baobab that can accommodate up to 40 people in its trunk. The hollow trunks are also used as storage barns, and some enterprising individuals have even opened shops within them.

Oh, what a wealth of fascinating stories there are about me! I am a much-talked-about tree.

Chapter 15

Whispers of Mortality

I often reflect on the fragility of life, even for a mighty tree like me. Though I have weathered many seasons, I know that my existence is not eternal.

I have seen the land around me change, as humans encroach upon my territory. Deforestation and urbanisation can alter the delicate balance of my ecosystem. Tourists often leave behind litter—plastic bottles, wrappers, and even broken glass—that mars the landscape and poses a threat to wildlife. As the world changes, I may find it increasingly difficult to survive.

In the heat of the dry season, I feel the weight of drought bear down on me. When the rains fail to come, my roots search deep into the earth, but sometimes even they can't find enough moisture. Without water, I grow weary, and my bark becomes brittle, leaving me vulnerable to the harshness of the world around me.

I have witnessed the creeping hand of disease. Fungal infections can invade my heartwood, causing it to rot from the inside out. What once was a strong trunk can become hollow and weak, making it difficult for me to stand firm against the winds that howl through the savannah

Pests, too, can be my undoing. Wood-boring beetles may tunnel into my bark, weakening my structure and leaving me open to further harm. They don't mean to do me harm; they are simply seeking shelter, but their presence can lead to my decline.

And when the storms rage and lightning splits the sky, I can feel the raw power of nature. A single strike can shatter my branches or set my bark ablaze, leaving me scarred or even lifeless.

So, while I am a symbol of endurance and strength, I am also a reminder that even the mightiest trees can face their end. Each day, I cherish my roots deep in the earth, the warmth of the sun on my leaves, and the beauty of the world, for I know that every moment is a precious gift.

Chapter 16

Sikiliza...Listen

Despite the hot sun shining down on me and the torrential rains accompanied by thunder and lightning, I stand erect and proud in all my glory—a sentinel watching the world change. How long will I be here before I fall into a heap on the ground that has sustained me and become one with it? A thousand years? Two thousand years? I do not know...

Every day is a new day. I wonder who will visit me today. Will I hear a new story to share with you?

I am the baobab, Mother of the Forest, a keeper of stories.

"Come, rest a while. Sit around me and listen to the winds of change blowing through," I whisper.

Beyond the Whispers…

Tarangire

Tarangire National Park, located in Northern Tanzania, East Africa, covers an area of 2,850 square kilometres, making it Tanzania's sixth-largest park. The park is defined by the giants of the plant and animal kingdom: the elephants and the ancient baobab trees. Its breathtaking landscape includes 500 square miles of woodlands, swamps, and plains dotted with gigantic baobabs and anthills.

Recipe for Candied *Mbuyu* (Baobab Candy)

Ingredients:

- ½ kg Baobab seeds
- 100 g Baobab powder
- 500 ml Water
- ½ kg Sugar
- ½ tablespoon Red food colouring
- Strawberry flavouring

Method:

1. In a sufuria (pan), pour the water.
2. Add the sugar, food colouring, and strawberry flavouring to the pan, and mix well.

3. Place the pan on medium heat and bring the mixture to a boil.
4. Allow the syrup to boil until it reaches a slightly sticky consistency. Be careful not to let it become too sticky, as this will result in hard candy.
5. Remove the pan from the heat. Gradually add the baobab seeds while stirring to ensure they are fully coated with the syrup.
6. Sprinkle some baobab powder into the mixture and continue stirring. This will help with the drying process.
7. Keep stirring to prevent the candy from clumping.
8. Once cooled, serve the candy or store it in airtight jars.

Swahili Terms and Sayings

- **Kuku mweupe ni hatari kwa usalama.**

  A white chicken is a danger to security and peace.

  (A white chicken stands out in the village, just like a stranger, which can easily upset the tranquillity of the community.)

- **Haraka haraka haina baraka.**

  Haste has no blessing.

- **Sifuri ubongo.**

  Zero brains.

- **Simba.**

  Lion.

- **Elimu haina mwisho.**

  Education has no end.

- **Heri yako, heri yangu.**

  Your happiness is my happiness.

- **Lala Salama**

  Sleep well

- **Mtalii.**

  Tourist.

- **Ndege**

  Birds

- **Rafiki**

  Friend

- **Sikiliza**

  Listen

- **Sopa.**

  Greeting in the Maa language spoken by the Maasai and other East African groups.

- **Ipa.**

  Response to the greeting.

- **Ole Sera!**

  Go in peace.

Here are some open-ended questions based on the book-

1. **How does the baobab tree in the story symbolize strength and resilience?**

    Explore how the tree is portrayed as a source of wisdom and endurance. What lessons can we learn from the baobab's ability to thrive in harsh conditions?

2. **In the book, the baobab communicates with the narrator. If you could have a conversation with a tree, what would you want to ask or tell it?**

    This question allows students to think creatively and reflect on nature's importance.

3. **What role does the natural environment play in the story, and how does it influence the characters' experiences?**

    Discuss how the setting (the forest, animals, or the baobab itself) shapes the characters' journey and the themes of the book.

4. **What do you think the title "Listen, Whispers the Baobab" means? Why do you think the author chose this title?**

    This encourages students to think critically about symbolism and the message of the story.

5. **If you were in the place of the main character, what would you have done differently when faced with the challenges in the story?**

This question invites students to consider problem-solving and different perspectives.

6. **What do you think the story teaches us about the relationship between humans and nature? How can we apply these lessons to our lives?**

This prompts students to reflect on the deeper themes of conservation and respect for the environment.

7. **The story talks about the beauty of the natural world through the eyes of children. How does the author use descriptive language to make nature come alive in the book?**

Students can discuss how imagery and descriptive writing bring the environment and the baobab to life.

8. **Do you think the baobab has a personality in the story? How would you describe it if you had to?**

This helps students think about personification and how the baobab acts as more than just a tree in the narrative.

9. **The book has themes of friendship and community. How do the characters support each other, and what can we learn from their relationships?**

Students can explore the themes of teamwork and empathy as they relate to the book's message.

10. **What did you learn about the importance of storytelling in the book? How do stories help us connect with each other and the world around us?**

This question encourages reflection on the power of storytelling in culture and tradition.

Additional Questions for Deeper Engagement:

11. **Imagine you could plant a special tree that people would gather around for years to come. What kind of stories or lessons would you want it to pass down?**

This question invites students to think about the kinds of values, wisdom, and messages they find meaningful and how they might share those with others.

12. **If you could spend a day in the baobab's world, what would you do, and what kind of creatures or people would you hope to meet?**

Encourages imagination and curiosity about the world around the baobab, and how the tree might serve as a bridge to discovering different animals, characters, or cultures.

Other Books by the Author

A Twinkle A Tear – Moments in a Mother's Life by Swarn Lamba is a heartfelt exploration of motherhood, capturing the emotional highs and lows that define the journey. Tears go with laughter in this collection of memories, as pain lies next to joy, and courage wraps around fears.

It shows the extraordinary way in which a mother has put one foot in front of the other through her grieving and loss. In the courage she shows and shares so openly.

The poems remind readers of the strength found in vulnerability and the beauty in life's simple, fleeting moments.

Let's Play Kanche and Other Traditional Games of India by Swarn Lamba is a vibrant celebration of India's rich heritage of folk games. The book brings to life the charm of timeless classics like Kanche, Gilli-Danda, Pittu, and Kho-Kho, games once played across villages and towns. Through detailed descriptions, Swarn revives these simple yet captivating pastimes, highlighting their cultural significance and the values they impart—teamwork, strategy, agility, and fun. By reconnecting readers with these traditional games, the book aims to educate younger generations about India's cultural roots while encouraging outdoor play, creativity, and community bonding in an increasingly digital age.